You Know You're in Hawai'i When...

Copyright © 2003 by Mutual Publishing
Illustrations copyright © by Roy Chang

No part of this book may be reproduced in any form or by any electronic or mechanical means, including information storage and retrieval devices or systems, without prior written permission from the publisher, except that brief passages may be quoted for reviews.

All rights reserved.

Library of Congress Catalog Card Number:

ISBN 1-56647-645-3

First Printing, November 2003
1 2 3 4 5 6 7 8 9

Mutual Publishing
1215 Center Street, Suite 210
Honolulu, Hawaii 96816
Ph: (808) 732-1709
Fax: (808) 734-4094
e-mail: mutual@mutualpublishing.com
www.mutualpublishing.com

Printed in Taiwan

You Know You're in Hawai'i When...

Don Chapman

Illustrations by Roy Chang

Mutual Publishing

In da beginning...

It began simply enough with a column in *MidWeek* leading up to Admissions/Statehood Day 2000, sometimes saluting, sometimes poking good-natured fun at the unique ways we do things in Hawai'i.

The first thing I learned after the wind dropped me here twenty-four years ago is that there are endless and delightful ways in which life in these islands is different from any other place on Earth, and that Hawai'i folks take great pride in celebrating the things that make us unique—from our foods and words to the way we greet friends and celebrate holidays.

The problem with that original column—titled "You Know You're in Hawai'i When…"—was that I had to leave so many little Hawai'i unique-isms out. This book provides an opportunity to add those and more.

That column seemed to strike a positive chord with readers, many of whom sent in their own observations of local culture.

A couple of readers also suggested that we post the column on *MidWeek*'s website for the benefit of Hawai'i ex-pats around the world. We did, and that's when "You Know You're in Hawai'i When…" took on a life of its own.

Before long it got copied and morphed into various emails zinging between Hawai'i residents and former residents and ex-visitors and people who just watched "Hawai'i Five-0" and "Magnum," and the emails apparently grew as people added their own responses before passing them along—including one called "You Know You're Chinese When…" (Perhaps I should start working on "You're Know You're Scottish/Tillamook Indian When…")

Anyway, early in 2003 another variation titled "You Know You're From Hawai'i When…" reached the folks at Mutual Publishing in Honolulu. They called around, inquiring if anyone knew where it began. John Heckathorn, *Honolulu Magazine* editor, said he thought it might be Chapman at *MidWeek*. And soon I heard from the detail-oriented—and gratefully so from my perspective—Jane Hopkins at Mutual.

So this is a book that would not have happened without the Web, the Internet and *MidWeek* readers, not to mention Mr. Heckathorn.

I owe a big "Mahalo!" to him as well to those *MidWeek* readers who responded so enthusiastically to the original column; to Perry Magpoc who did the Website posting; to those who gave it new permutations and passed it along; to the folks at Mutual Publishing for having the vision to turn a column/email into a book; and especially to friends such as, Rick Ornellas, Lynne Matsuo Chang and the late Henry Loui and their 'ohana, who with open hearts and homes welcomed this "Coast haole" and shared the intricacies of local culture, language and cuisine. This book would not have been possible without their patient friendship, not to mention their translations.

I'm also pleased that Roy Chang, *MidWeek*'s award-winning editorial cartoonist, was chosen to create the illustrations for *You Know You're in Hawai'i When...* The first time I saw his 'toons, the thing that hit me was his just-right eye for capturing Hawai'i people, scenes and sensibilities as no other artist can, combined with a sly, kolohe sense of humor. That's why *MidWeek* grabbed him, and those qualities show through here.

Thanks, too, to Terri Hefner for her eagle-eye copy editing.

Back to the beginning: You're definitely in Hawai'i when none of your friends knows when Admissions/Statehood Day is. I asked a bunch of locally born folks and a bunch of immigres—got a bunch of answers, none of which was the correct one: August 21.

By the way, *You Know You're in Hawai'i When...* was written with Hawaiian music playing in the background. It might be best read that way too.

Don Chapman
Kane'ohe, June 2003

On the street where you live, porches are covered with slippahs...

Neighbors share mango, avocado and lychee from their trees...

Everybody lives on the sunny side of the street...

"My kids said give you some lychee from our yard. I think they like eat mangos now."

"Okay, we found Diamond Head and Ewa. I still can't find Mauka or Makai."

Nobody is exactly sure which way North is...

"Go ewa 'til you get to da kine, then makai, and bum-by you stay there" is considered giving explicit directions...

There are so many ways to compliment good food:

Onolicious!...

Da buggah was ono!...

Oh, brah, broke da mout'...

"Sir, the manager sends this complimentary SECOND SERVING just so you would stop that."

"Hea! No, I nevah sip from yours!"

The state dog is the pit bull...

The state beverage is fruit punch...

The state anthem is "It's Aloha Friday"...

When you greet a friend, your chin nods up: "Howzit?"...

Everybody is part of an ethnic minority...

Saying "Eh!" constitutes major oratory filled with profound implications...

["Quick! What's the response for this word — 'HOWZIT'?"]

"Sir, the breathalizer result says you're not drunk, but you sure ate a lot of spicy pupus! Care for some mints?"

You get cuttlefish breath...

You get kim chee breath...

You get natto breath...

The most important thing to know about a person is where they went to high school...

Second is the year they wen' grad...

Third, who's their cousins...

"So, oh.... what school you went?"

Your cousin is Japanese-Chinese-French-Filipino-Korean-Scottish-Portuguese-Hawaiian, plus some other stuff too manini to mention...

You once dated another cousin without even knowing it until later!...

It's bad luck to carry pork over the Pali...

It's bad luck to whistle after dark...

A lava rock gives you chickenskin...

"Kimo, try look in dah rearview mirror. Is dat da same 'ol lady hitchhiker we picked up down da road?"

You know exactly why they call it Point Panic...

You cruise Sandy's (not Sandy Beach)...

Da wind was so strong at Sandy's, auwe, my kite wen' buckaloose...

To impress the wahine on your first date, you wear your bestest shorts...

Plus the new Surfah rubbah slippahs...

And leave your favorite puka-puka shirt until you know her better...

"We got another delivery tomorrow!"

Spam is for special occasions...

White rice is a sacrament...

The last bag of poi is worth fighting for...

Shopping is a therapeutic art form...

Stopping to smell the flowers can take all day...

You're officially "old" the first time you get called "auntie" or "uncle"...

"Come down meet me. I'm just relaxing at the mall."

"Ho, Tutu! You strong enough to lift me even with all dat bracelets?"

You've got a "slippah tan"...

You wonder how that wahine can even lift her arm with all those gold bracelets jangling on her wrist...

You tell your honey you're coming "shtraight" home...

You park your car on the "shtreet"...

Your keeds give you "shtress"...

"Oh, cannot go. My faddah said to 'shtay' home cuz I gotta 'shtudy.'"

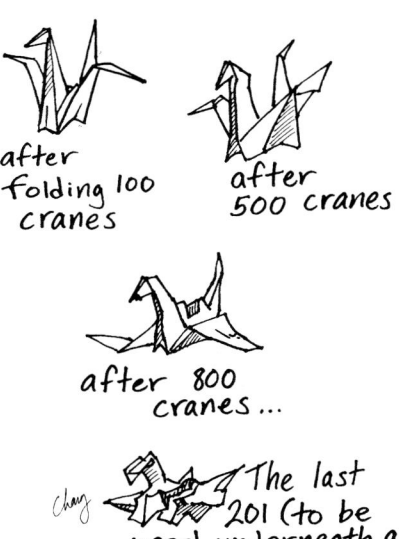

You go into debt paying for your 1-year-old's baby luau...

Fireworks are bigger on New Year's Eve than the 4th of July...

Your fingers cramp up folding origami for your best friend's wedding...

Basic condiments on your kitchen table include shoyu, chili pepper water, ketchup, Hawaiian salt...

You can never have enough rice cookers...

There's nothing that can't be improved by frying it...

"Nice poster, but that's not how the food pyramid goes!"

"Brah, gotta go home fo' watch on top."

The UH campus is located on "the Manoa side" of Oʻahu...

"Brah" is not a female undergarment...

You watch UH Wahine volleyball "on top the TV"...

Your second home is the beach...

Dining out means a plate lunch...

Official footwear is barefoot...

"Next time you ask me out to dinner in Waikiki, I'm choosing a place!"

"A'com! Everybody stay telling me I look like dat buggah."

You're fluent in shaka—a shaka for any occasion, any emotion...

Kamehameha Day is a paid holiday...

You know this one guy just like Bu La'ia. Maybe t'ree...

When the temperature drops into the 70s, you get out the heavy quilts...

Anything above 80, "Oh da hot already!"...

A cold shower means the end of a day at the beach...

"Mom! Dad! Somebody? Anybody?!"

Graduates risk suffocation—or neck injury, whichever comes first—by flower lei...

You offer a toast with "Okole maluna!"...

Or "Ban-zai! Ban-zai! Ban-zai!"...

Mother's Day is special for local boys—it signals the start of South Shore surf season...

Summer starts with the first bon dance...

Winter begins when the first monster swell pounds the North Shore...

"Humbug! Just when swells get gnarly here, I gotta head back North to work."

"Ha! I saw your eyes moving down!"

The name Duke means royalty...

The ukulele is a classical instrument...

You really do keep your eyes on the hula girl's hands, mostly...

The TV weather wahine predicts "mauka showers"...

It rains buckets on your reunion and everyone agrees it's "a blessing"...

If it doesn't rain Saturday, you're "going go for lawnmower da grass"...

"C'mon, Brah!... JAN-KEN-PO one mo' time!"

You get stink-eye...

An' wot, bodda you?...

Eh, you know what I like do?...

You can't visit a friend without bringing food or flowers...

You can't say hello or good-bye without a kiss...

You can't leave a party without helping to clean up...

"A hui hou aku, sistah!"

No matter how old you are, if you catch your friend making even a little mistake, you tell 'em "Hanaokolele!"...

And no matter how old you are, eh, no make-A...

A dinner of poke, soba, adobo, char siu and kal-bi doesn't seem like international cuisine...

It wouldn't be a meal without rice, mac salad, poi, cone sushi and sweet bread...

"Actually, we prefer to call this international ethnic cuisine."

"Pau" is not a Batman fight scene sound effect...

That surfer didn't flip when he wiped out, "Bruddah wen' huli"...

"Shoots" is a two-syllable word...

Nobody knows where the fast lane is on the H-1...

The interstate highway system won't get you into the next county...

A skateboard is public transportation...

"Okay, maybe moving to the left lane wasn't a good idea."

"Yeah, I know it's kapakahi, but I know where everything stay!"

Everything is all kapakahi…

When things go all hemajang, you feel kinda all bus' up…

When you go moe-moe, you wake up with maka-pia-pia…

"You like beef?" has nothing to do with what's for dinner...

Macaroni salad comes with potatoes...

A boy becomes a man when he learns to barbecue...

"What? Am I supposed to use da 'FORCE'?"

"May as well eat some while we wait for da rescue chopper. Watchu' figgah?"

People gladly risk their lives for a little seaweed and opihi...

You know two people named Junior Boy and three named Honey Girl...

Bruddah-Bruddah lets you cut in front of him in traffic...

The sight of a gecko on the bedroom ceiling evokes screams usually reserved for Godzilla and Frankenstein, together...

And isn't it something how cockroaches and rubber slippers just seem to go together?...

"Suddenly we saw a light come on and THIS happened!"

"And to our jar, we'll add..."

Portuguese sausage is part of a balanced breakfast...

Azuki beans are the perfect condiment for ice cream...

The best cooks use a lot of mayonnaise...

Traditional Thanksgiving fare includes lomi-lomi, mahi-mahi and turkey-turkey...

The Ala Moana Center Santa brings sentimental tears to your eyes...

You always barbecue on Christmas Eve...

"Don't worry, Sweetie! It's still October. We can keep coming back to visit Santa!"

Your auntie makes the best picko'd mango...

Your uncle plays slack key...

Your tutu has seen the nightmarchers and converses with Pueo the owl...

A trip of any length requires a cache of crackseed and arare...

When you travel, you bring back omiyage...

The best part of any vacation is coming home...

"Dang! Crackseeds! Cuttlefish! Crackers! You must be from HAWAI'I."

"Honolulu City Lights" always brings a happy, grateful tear...

You're welcomed into the 'ohana...

A stranger shares aloha...

And when that happens, you know you're in Hawai'i. Fo' shuah. I no keed you. Garans ball bearins.

About the Author

Award-winning writer/editor Don Chapman, a native of Oregon, has been entertaining and informing Hawai'i readers since he was "fresh off the boat" from the *San Jose Mercury News* in 1979. He wrote a daily column for the *Honolulu Advertiser* for thirteen years, since 1994 has been the editor of *MidWeek,* recently judged Hawai'i's best non-daily newspaper by the Hawai'i Publishers Association, and is in his third year of writing daily, serialized novels for the *Honolulu Star-Bulletin.* The father of two Scottish-Japanese-Native Hawaiian-Native American-Portuguese-Chinese-French-English children, he resides in Kane'ohe and plays conga drums rather badly.

About the Illustrator

Roy Chang has been the regular Editorial Cartoonist for *Midweek* since August 2002. A graduate from Moanalua High, he attended the California College of Arts in Oakland and the Academy of Art College in San Francisco where he earned his BFA in Illustration. From 1993 to 2002, he worked as the Editiorial Cartoonist for U.H.'s "Ka Leo O Hawai'i" winning several awards year after year for Outstanding Editorial Cartoon by the Hawai'i Newpaper Agency and Board of Publications. Most recently, he won a Pa'i Award for his *Midweek* cartoon work. Roy is also an art teacher and is finishing a Masters degree in Education. His cartoons and illustrations have appeared in *The Price of Paradise, Hawai'i 2020, The Good Life,* as well as in *Honolulu Magazine, Honolulu Weekly, Hawai'i Business News,* and the *Honolulu Star Bulletin.* He's single, oh, so single. Roy resides in Salt Lake and drives a new beetle named Herbie. Inspired from an art project he led last school year with his 7th and 8th grade students, he is now writing and illustrating his first novel.

Grandmother = Love

The C.R. Gibson Company
Norwalk, Connecticut

Copyright © MCMLXXIX by
The C.R. Gibson Company
Norwalk, Connecticut
All rights reserved
Printed in the United States of America
ISBN: 0-8378-5021-5

Small wonder we love our grandchildren.
They are our immortality.

                                                PHYLLIS McGINLEY

THE GRANDMOTHER EXPERIENCE

For me and for every woman I know, no matter how many of our friends have arrived there before us, no matter what we have expected or been told to expect, becoming a grandmother has been a totally new and wonderful but also somewhat strange experience for which nothing seems to have prepared us in advance. And as the children grow and change, we are constantly discovering new aspects of our role in their lives and their effect on ours, even — to our surprise — new aspects of ourselves.

RUTH GOODE

Toddling, first tasting snow, each grandchild re-creates our world of wonder.

I watch my granddaughter walking from the sofa to the chair. When she falls down, she thinks it highly amusing. Muffin (her name is Alice Elizabeth and this is too much right now for so small a person), Muffin is now exhibiting what I have read was the first stage of the development of man, when he got up from all fours and walked erect. Muffin had, heretofore, traveled rapidly and expertly on all fours. Suddenly she decided to change her method of locomotion, and now there is the miracle of learning to balance, and to walk. She falls down, she weaves a lot, but she walks.

    She enjoys this erect position so much that she insists on standing up in her feeding chair while she has her meals. When Muffin is in the mood, she flings her spoon down. Meals are followed by a mopping-up process both on Muffin and the floor and the kitchen counter. Muffin finds this delightful. In fact, Muffin finds most of life highly amusing.

    Muffin, at a year and a half, had her first experience with pure country snow. In her blue bunny suit, she looked like an indigo bunting as she went out.

    At first, Muffin just stood and stared. Then she sat down in a soft drift, ate some. Then she made miniature brooms of her arms and swept. All the time she said "Whoo — whoo — whoo" like a tiny blue owl.

When I thought of the world opening up for my granddaughter, the immeasurable experiences, and the things to learn, I felt awed. She was like the first human being in the first snow. Somewhere along the line, we lose the sense of wonder. We look out, and sigh, and say, "It's snowing again."

For adults, it means, in the country, shoveling, stalled cars, more wood-lugging, being housebound until the road crews finally get through. It means empty bird feeders until we make a path. It means an added load. But to Muffin it meant a strange new wonder. Her hands were full of sparkles and then they were gone.

As I watched her being peeled off like an onion, I wished we might all keep the sense of wonder she now has when all life is a mystery, and a whoo — whoo — whoo kind of thing.

GLADYS TABER

THE LADY WHO LIVED THROUGH WINTER

One of my neighbors sometimes sits for an hour in drizzle and damp, watching what the birds are up to. Then he comes to tell me and, while he's at it, he points out colors in the fire, or shows me a pebble, saying, "Now isn't that pretty!" Musing, he once remarked, "I guess I'm an appreciatin' kind of fella."

And I'm an appreciatin' kind of gal. Only a few weeks ago, I was standing in the middle of a snowbound patch of mud, appreciatin'.

Ooze had seeped into my boots. Ice-melt from the trees was leaking onto my hat. The sun was far away, a bleached circle in the sky. In the whole yard I could see but one bird, a bedraggled winter robin hopping forlornly through slush. But this all seemed *beautiful* to me! I'd come out my door expecting yet another day of winter; instead, I'd sunk three inches into spring.

The gray and damp were profligate with promises. The thaw meant softening, and warming, and greening; grass where mud was, buttercups where snow was thinning. There'd be buds along these branches! The robin would fall in love and preen his feathers — and there'd be lilacs! And ladybugs, and ten-speed bicycles tick-ticking by, and curtains astir at open windows!

I looked happily down at the mud, and up, and all around. I could have danced right there, in my galoshes! Spring! Oh, my — how I appreciated it!

JOAN MILLS

BUT OH! WITH LOVE

Nor what I am,
Nor what I say,
Will matter much
Beyond today,
And so it is
With this in mind,
I get on well
With humankind,
With rainy weather
And with pain,
With joy and sorrow,
Loss and gain,
But Oh! with Love,
I beg, I borrow,
Today, tomorrow
And tomorrow!

GLADYS McKEE IKER

BEGINNINGS

In April come beginnings,
rebirth, with grass cool green,
and sunlight playing long at noon
to kindle leaves with sheen.

A welcome month of miracles,
from melting beds of snow
to color warming winter's land,
that crocuses might grow.

And tenderly the springtime seeds
that nature sprouts anew
will blossom reawakening
within my spirit, too.

VIRGINIA COVEY BOSWELL

VELVET SHOES

Let us walk in the white snow
    In a soundless space;
With footsteps quiet and slow,
    At a tranquil pace,
    Under veils of white lace.

I shall go shod in silk,
    And you in wool,
White as a white cow's milk,
    More beautiful
    Than the breast of a gull.

We shall walk through the still town
    In a windless peace;
We shall step upon white down,
    Upon silver fleece,
    Upon softer than these.

We shall walk in velvet shoes:
    Wherever we go
Silence will fall like dews
    On white silence below.
    We shall walk in the snow.

ELINOR WYLIE

What is a Grandmother really like? According to Lee Parr McGrath and Joan Scobey, on-target observations from grandchildren tell it like it is.

A grandmother will rush you to the hospital if you scratch your finger. They are serusely disturbed about grems.

EDDIE

What is a Grandmother? Some one who tells you the *bad* things your mother did when she was a little girl.

LOUISE

A grandmother can tell stories and ferrytails 24 hours a day, but now I'm to big for grandmother stories.

JENNY

Granmothers do their best to help out people. They are also very clean and reverent.

BRADLEY

My grandmother is a groovy person. She rides a honda. She is married to a grandfather.

TIMMY

I sometimes have to protect my grandmother when my mother scolds her.

GRACE

Grandmothers say they have very good memeriers
but they can't rember how old they are.

TRACY

A grandma is made to spoil you and save you
from your parents.

ANDY

Grandmothers play with you whether they are busy or
not That's why a grandmother is my kind of person

MARGARET

All I can say is that a grandmother loves you a lot
but you have to be good.

PETE

WHEN GRANDMAMA WAS YOUNG

Once upon a time
When grandmama was young,
Foxes played on bagpipes,
Raccoons beat on drums,
Mice danced minuets,
Squirrels two-stepped gaily,
And the unmarried cottontails
Gave tea parties daily.

ELIZABETH COATSWORTH

GRANDMOTHER GOES BAREFOOT

I always promised myself that when I became a grandmother I would do it up brown, dress like one, act like one, and sit peacefully in rocking chairs knitting tiny garments for the latest babies. Unfortunately, I find that it's much harder than I thought to buckle down and wear violet print dresses, gun-metal stockings, and black health shoes the way Baba did. I'm sorry to report that I wear shorts, old shirts cast off by my sons, and frequently no stockings or shoes at all. I never knit garments, tiny or otherwise, but I can cook and make bread, which is something. Anyway, Deborah and Pieter think grandmothers wear shorts and go barefoot and do the cooking.

JANET GILLESPIE

MOTHER'S LAMENT

*(Who is Stuck at Home While Grandma
Is Out Having the Time of Her Life)*

*Where have all the Grandmas gone?
A lobbying in Washington,
Back to work and back to school,
To Peace Corps posts in Istanbul,
To regional meetings on woman's rights,
To seminars to raise their sights,
To the tennis courts and to the races,
To Thebes and Antibes and faraway places,
To castles in Spain and to Congress —*

Oh dear, why couldn't she wait for us!

BARBARA SHOOK HAZEN

A grandmother doesn't have to do anything except be there . . . Everybody should try to have one, especially if you don't have television, because grandmas are the only grown-ups who have got time.

PATSY GRAY

All the clichés work: The pleasure without the trouble, the charming smile that draws you back and back and back. The mystery still pervades your wonder at how that new little body and mind integrate every sensation and experience into new personhood.

FLORENCE D. SHELLEY

ANY AGE WE PLEASE

Walking down a residential street the other day, I came across an older woman playing hopscotch with a little girl. Fascinated, I stopped to watch. They seemed to be having so much fun. Besides thoroughly enjoying herself, the hopping woman showed considerably more vigor and agility than I, who must have been at least 10 years her junior.

When the game was finished, the little girl clapped her hands. "I won. I won. But you almost beat me, Grandma."

"Next time, maybe I will." The grandmother turned toward me, a twinkle in her eyes. "I haven't had so much fun since I tried to ride my youngest grandson's skateboard. Almost every day my daughter says to me, 'Mama, be your age.' But I tell her I'll be any age I please."

Continuing on my way, I couldn't get the incident out of my mind. If there is one rebuke we have received from childhood on, and which we consistently resent, it is "be your age." Why should those of us who have lived through most of the ages of man be expected to cast off our earlier skins and emerge denuded of whatever we have found worthwhile in life merely to conform to society's concept of how older people should behave? Why can't we be any age we please?

How glorious it would feel to be the age of a child again, to experience the sense of wonder and curiosity and hopefulness we knew before the smog of cynicism polluted our ideals, and sometimes our ethics. Very young children love freely, forgive easily, learn for learning's sake — are these traits too juvenile for mature people? Children have endless enthusiasm, energy, trustfulness, generosity and resourcefulness. If we seek to retain even a couple of these qualities, are we behaving childishly?

The teen years have always been rebellious years, but who can say that rebellion is incompatible with maturity? Is it immature to rebel against a double standard from which adults preach one thing to youth and practice something entirely different themselves? Is it immature to denounce the hypocritical, the superficial, the corrupt? One reason why teenagers often communicate better with their grandparents than with their parents is because they, too, resent being forced into a mold. If we can feel empathy with the young, then surely we can be a young age, if we please, and not feel guilty about it, either.

There are other ages we can please to be. The age of humor, for instance, which is no chronological age but a fast disappearing way of looking at life, a lightness of spirit which too often dissipates as we grow older. To treasure a sense of humor is to drink forever at the fountain of youth.

Or we can be the age of exuberance, the effervescence of all ages with its bubbling life force which spills over and regenerates all whom it touches.

We can even try for the age of adventure and the next time someone asks "Shall we?" answer "Let's" without first thinking about all the reasons why we should not.

LEE NEVILLE

FROM GRANDMOTHER

My gifts to my grandchild
    are few and spare,
A rocking horse
    And a rocking chair,
A handful of songs
    That her mother knew,
And stories about
    How her mother grew.

"Once, on the farm,
    When the weather was cold,
We sawed big logs
    That your mother rolled."
Earnestly staring,
    Linda sees
A towhead mother
    With skinned-up knees.

"She braided the horses's
    Mane and tail —
Kept pet green frogs
    In a shiny pail."
Linda, through such a
    Telescope,
Looks back with wonder,
    Ahead with hope.

LoVERNE BROWN

WHAT GRANDPARENTS CAN GIVE

Grandparents can offer a strong relationship to their grandchildren. Their love and devotion are often as intense as the love and devotion parents give. And because grandparents don't have to feel the responsibility for shaping their grandchildren's characters every minute of the day as parents do, I think they are able to enjoy their grandchildren more. In turn the children are able to enjoy their grandparents. Grandparents usually have more leisure too, so they can translate their devotion into such time-consuming activities as reading aloud, playing house and making excursions to zoos, museums and the beach.

From both theoretical and practical points of view, good grandparents have considerably more to offer than baby sitters with equally sound characters. Grandparents' love has that glowing, doting and possessive flavor that is exactly what gives children their special confidence in and love for them.

BENJAMIN SPOCK, M.D.

HUGS, KISSES AND CHICKEN SOUP

It's sensational, this being a grandma, and I wouldn't miss it for the world. I know from the beautiful extravagant presents my nongrandma friends shower on this baby that I'm on to something special.

I'm the one who remembers the words to "Did You Ever See a Lassie?" or the words to "Patty Cake." I'm the one who says don't worry, or do, over some unusual development. I'm the one who bakes the cookies or the birthday cake and brings the stew and reads the books at cranky time — when I'm not writing a book myself or going off to Europe to enjoy myself with my attractive husband.

I'm the one who knows what it's like to juggle sleepless nights, new anxiety over being responsible for a tiny human, a ton of physical drudgery and the uneasy moments between new parents when their lovers' life seems hostage to this demanding little person.

The distance of a generation is what I give, what grandmas give, along with hugs, kisses and chicken soup, even when they are dressed up to look like modern grandmothers.

FLORENCE D. SHELLEY

SUNDAY DINNER

this early afternoon

    the chicken
is in the pan
        and the yams
are boiling in the pot

a lot of work for sunday
           dinner
  and a little time before
the biscuits and the greens

beans
are a snap for me
at the kitchen table
      as grandma sits
         and knits
         and
              knits

and tells a sunday dinner story
about marching women long ago
        and brave old songs

        and grandma knits
          and   knits

ARNOLD ADOFF

*Always and in all ways, it was grandmother.
A loving tribute.*

First grandchildren are important, and I was the lucky one in our family to be my grandmother's first grandchild. My grandparents lived nearby which was fortunate. Whenever childhood crises occurred — it was easy to flee to the next neighborhood, find grandmother and pour out one's troubles over milk and cookies at the kitchen table. She was *always there.*

When school started, it was my grandmother who bought the First Day dress and the new hair ribbon. She was there to wave goodbye and inquire, since cafeterias were as yet unknown, if I had a treat for recess. If I were lucky she might be there when I arrived home, bursting with importance and self-consciously toting a huge selection of brand-new books. My grandmother would listen sympathetically as I grimly described my horrendous day and clucked at the incredible amount of homework. ("You have so much!")

At the week's end, my bag was packed and I walked (saving the trolley fare meant an ice cream cone on the way) to my grandmother's house where there occurred a reunion that would have been more appropriate if I'd been away a year rather than just a day or two. Weekends were when my grandmother prepared dinner for three with as much thought as if company were coming, as indeed it was. *I* was the company! There was always the assurance of getting one's favorite things, like creamed chipped beef over boiled new potatoes, not plain old toast. There were freshly baked pies, homemade succotash, preserves, jams and pickles and always, for Sunday breakfast, "fried doughs," the New England descendant of the English crumpet and the antecedent of the Southern 'hush puppy.' On the previous evening, there would have been a visit to the neighborhood movie where the local pianist regaled us with the "Blue Danube" before the theater darkened. Those were the days of the cliff-hanging serials and, over dinner, discussion would center on how our heroine would escape the peril she had encountered the previous week. Dishes were done in a hurry; my grandparents were as eager to be off as I.

MARY MUNGER LUKE

CHILDREN AND OTHER CREATURES

Children
(like other creatures)
Love the sun,
Like to lie down
In the grass
And roll
(like cats)
Quite free,
Love to sing
(like birds)
And (like ants)
Love a sugary thing.
And (like children)
Love to bring
Gifts to grandparents.

FELICE HOLMAN

SMASHED POTATOES:
A KID'S-EYE VIEW OF THE KITCHEN

Jane G. Martel, a schoolteacher in Winchester, Mass., asked for recipes from nursery-school and kindergarten children. Here are some of the choicest morsels:

SCRAMBLED EGGS
5 pounds of boiled bacon
2 pounds of eggs
3 pounds of ginger ale
1 fat
8 gallon of salt
4 pounds of pepper
1 knife of butter

First you open the eggs with your mittens. Use only the inside. Throw the rest in the sink. Put the eggs in a 10 pound can and cook the bacon in a plastic pan. Get your pan real hot. If you get your pan hot first, you only have to cook for 2 minutes. But if the pan is not hot, you have to cook for 3 hours.

Eat them in the morning or in the afternoon. And you will sure need some orange juice after.

A WHOLE TURKEY

1 big bag full of a whole turkey (get the kind with no feathers on, not the kind the Pilgrims ate).

A giant lump of stuffin'

1 squash pie

1 little fancy dish of sour berries

1 big fancy dish of a vegetable mix

20 dishes of all different candies, chocolate balls, cherry balls and peanuts

Get up when the alarm says to and get busy fast. Unfold the turkey and open up the holes. Push in the stuffin' for a couple hours. You have to pin the stuffin' to the turkey or I suppose it would get out. Get the kitchen real hot, and from there on you just cook turkey.

Then you put the vegetables in the cooker — and first put one on top, and next put one on the bottom, and then one in the middle. That makes a vegetable mix. Put 2 red things of salt all in it and 2 red things of water also. Cook them to just ½ of warm.

Put candies all around the place, and when the company comes put on your red apron.

WHAT GRANDMA SAYS

When I wiggle,
When I squirm,
Father says
I'm like a worm.
But grandma says
That isn't true.
I'm doing what
A child must do.

When it's bedtime
And I scowl,
Mother says
I'm like an owl.
But grandma says
It isn't true.
I'm doing what
Most children do.

B. J. LEE

grandma (grand'ma), n. The mother of one's father or mother.

The role of a grandmother has never been really defined. Some sit in rockers, some sky dive, some have careers. Others clean ovens. Some have white hair. Others wear wigs. Some see their grandchildren once a day (and it's not enough). Others, once a year (and that's too much).

Once I conducted an interesting survey among a group of eight-year-olds on grandmas. I asked them three questions. One, what is a grandmother? Two, what does she do? And three, what is the difference between a grandmother and a mother?

To the first question, the answers were rather predictable. "She's old (about eighty), helps around the house, is nice and kind, and is Mother's mother or Father's mother, depending on the one who is around the most."

To the second question, the answers again were rather obvious. Most of them noted grandmothers knit, do dishes, clean the bathroom, make good pies; and a goodly number reveled in the fact that Grandma polished their shoes for them.

It was the third question that stimulated the most reaction from them. Here is their composite of the differences between a mother and a grandmother. "Grandma has gray hair, lives alone, takes me places and lets me go into her attic. She can't swim. Grandma doesn't spank you and stops Mother when she does. Mothers scold better and more. Mothers are married. Grandmas aren't.

"Grandma goes to work and my mother doesn't do anything. Mom gives me shots, but Grandma gives me frogs. Grandma lives faraway. A mother you're born from. A grandmother gets married to a grandfather first, a mother to a father last.

"Grandma always says, 'Stay in, it's cold outside,' and my mother says, 'Go out, it's good for you.' "

And here's the clincher. Out of thirty-nine children queried, a total of thirty-three associated the word "love" with Grandma. One summed up the total very well with, "Grandma loves me all the time."

ERMA BOMBECK

All virtues are good, but some virtues seem more virtuous than others. Take generosity, for instance. It smells sweeter than lilies of the valley, never goes out of style, and who has it needs very little else.

PHYLLIS McGINLEY

LETTER TO MY GRANDMOTHER

Dear Granny,

Ever since Gramps died, I have thought more and more about the important role the two of you have played in my life. I too am growing older: At 32 I am much more aware than I was in my 20s of the ways in which I have been shaped by the past.

There you are, you see, in my first conscious memory. My mother left me — I don't remember her leaving me before then, though she surely must have done so — and came home with a baby brother. My parents brought Robbie home to your old house with the wonderful attic, not to our small apartment in the city. I suppose I must have been jealous, but I don't remember that either. I do remember your talking to me before they came home and telling me I would always be special because I was the *first* grandchild.

I often start thinking about you when I am standing next to a kitchen stove. Like you (and unlike my mother), I love to cook. I inherited many of my favorite recipes from you. I understand exactly why I know how to fix potatoes 20 different ways and why my health-food-freak friends are horrified at the starch and calorie content of my meals. You were the daughter of German immigrants, and you found it hard to imagine a meal without potatoes. I too feel a growl of protest in my stomach when I confront a meal without potatoes — that is, unless there is some pasta in sight. I understand the potatoes, but I can't quite figure out how your German heritage taught you to make such terrific spaghetti sauce. I make mine just the way you did, simmering it for hours with lots of fresh garlic and onions and tomatoes and bay leaves. I've been to Italy six times in the last ten years, Gran, and there isn't any better sauce than yours. The meatballs I make with fresh beef and pork, ground by the butcher right in front of my eyes. *Never buy any chopped meat unless you've seen what went into the grinder, Susie.* I never do.

Like you, I consider food an important expression of love, friendship and hospitality. In my home I feed only my real friends. Apart from making love, there's nothing I like to do more with a man I love than to cook for him.

I know the equation between food and love can be overdone. Since my mother and I have both grown up enough to talk about *her* childhood, I have learned that she was once fat and blames you for stuffing her when she was little. That's the difference between being a parent and a grandparent. A grandmother can stuff a grandchild with food and love without the awful weight of responsibility that makes a parent the target of old childhood fears and resentments — even though the parent may be 70 and the child 50. The relationship between a grandparent and a grandchild offers one of the few opportunities for people to give and receive unquestioning, undemanding love.

SUSAN JACOBY

THE HOUSE PLANTS

The house plants always have
                a look
Of prisoners staring through
                the bars,
They miss the air and
                grass and stars.

And so I always talk
                with them,
And touch them with
                my softest hand,
To show them that I understand.

                ELIZABETH COATSWORTH

LOVE

What is love
  but a heart grown tall
Reaching beyond
life's grey stone wall.

What is love
  but a heart grown strong,
Lifting a burden with a song.

What is love
  but a heart whose smiles
Give help and courage
  on rugged miles.

What is love
  but a heart whose calm
Pours out to all a quiet psalm,
And human hearts are fed
Manna and they are comforted.

BETTIE PAYNE WELLES

SOMETHING REALLY NEW

Our grandchildren expand and enhance our lives in ways that reach deep. They reach back into our past and far into our future. They re-create old joys for us, and promise ever new ones as they grow. As for our present, they can enrich the hours and days if we wish, and as much as we wish. As grandparents we have the choice, always, of how much or how little we are involved with them, and even a little involvement — the one or two visits a year if they live far away — can bring very special pleasures.

Each one of our grandchildren is a fresh, unique experience, a new personality, a small but definite individual with whom we can forge a bond. If we are shy with babies, soon enough we find them toddlers, conversationalists on the telephone, crayon artists sending us pictures, school children writing us awkwardly formed words in block letters and original spellings, teen-agers confiding to us their adolescent joys and griefs. We can enter their lives at any stage with which we feel comfortable. And we enter with an ideal introduction, a passport second only to that of their parents. We are their grandparents.

But there is much more that our grandchildren do for us. They rekindle for us the spirit of play, the child's sense of adventure and discovery. Grandparents are always being told that they are living history to their grandchildren, that they give the children the reassurance of their roots, the strengthening awareness of continuity. For me and many grandmothers I have talked to, it works the other way as well. They give *us* continuity. They link us to our own motherhood and childhood years, to our parents and grandparents and the stories we remember of times even earlier than those. And they link us to the future as well. They give us a vested interest in the world in which they will live. They make us aware of the world in which we are living today and helping to create for tomorrow.

And all this at our own choice. We choose how far and how deep our grandparenthood will take us. For perhaps the first time in our lives, as grandparents we have the freedom to take as little or as much as we desire out of this new facet of living that our grandchildren bring to us.

RUTH GOODE

MEDITATIONS

Have a mental garage sale. Get rid of all the thoughts you don't really need.

Appreciate a sunset. Maybe even God has a need for approval.

A way of avoiding wrinkles: Don't look for them so hard.

Women, like wine, are tastier for a little aging. Help spread the rumor.

Everyone you know can tell you how terrible things are. Be original. Learn to see the bright side.

See crabgrass as an assertion of spirit on the part of weeds.

GWEN DAVIS

Full, golden days — a fortune in happiness.

THE FORTUNE

Day's end. A Midas sack of cloud has spilled this
wealth of radiance down the chutes of air into the
river. Let me gather gold

seeping at large as though the treasure welled up
from water. Whom to thank for the rare day's end a
Midas sack of cloud has spilled?

The giver's gone. A sun's dropped from the world.
Let me surviving plunge my vision bare into the river.
Let me gather gold

to keep at heart. The night is forecast cold. Hot rays of
noon worked westward to prepare day's end. A Midas
sack of cloud has spilled

sheer again. Here's an inheritance that's spelled *light*.
I claim it, searching deep as I dare into the river. Let
me gather gold

against a pauper dark. Here, stranger, hold my hand.
I'm rescuing — so enriched I stare — day's end a Midas
sack of cloud has spilled into the river. Let me gather
gold.

NORMA FARBER

A grandmother is hope for the future and eyes into the past.

This is our fourth four-generation summer. Four Junes ago Mother's namesake and first great-grandchild, Madeleine, was born. We call her Léna, to avoid confusion in this household of Madeleines. Charlotte, the second great-granddaughter, was born fourteen months later. My mother is very proud of being the Great-grandmother.

But she is hardly the gentle little old lady who sits by the fireside and knits. My knowledge of her is limited by my own chronology; I was not around for nearly forty years of her life, and her premotherhood existence was exotic and adventurous; in the days before planes she traveled by camel and donkey; she strode casually through a world which is gone and which I will never see except through her eyes.

MADELEINE L'ENGLE

OUR HOPE FOR TOMORROW

Life is a continuum, a stream, and all that we have ever been is part of what we are now, and will be. Seeing children, loving their presence in my world, watching child nature express itself, is a constant reminder of the child within, which is my humanity, my possibilities for further growing. When I am happiest, most fulfilled, most loving, there is a child being nourished in a secret garden inside of me, a child I have not forgotten to love and to cherish, until death.

That is what all species of babies are about — the miracle of miracles, the rebirth of life. And nothing in our world can help us rekindle hope as much as a human child. A baby is the ultimate antidote to human terror and despair; it is our only hope, each new baby representing the possibility of tomorrow and of something good to come.

EDA LE SHAN

Our first grandchild is the herald of a new phase in our lives, and every grandchild that comes after will reaffirm the wonder of it.

RUTH GOODE

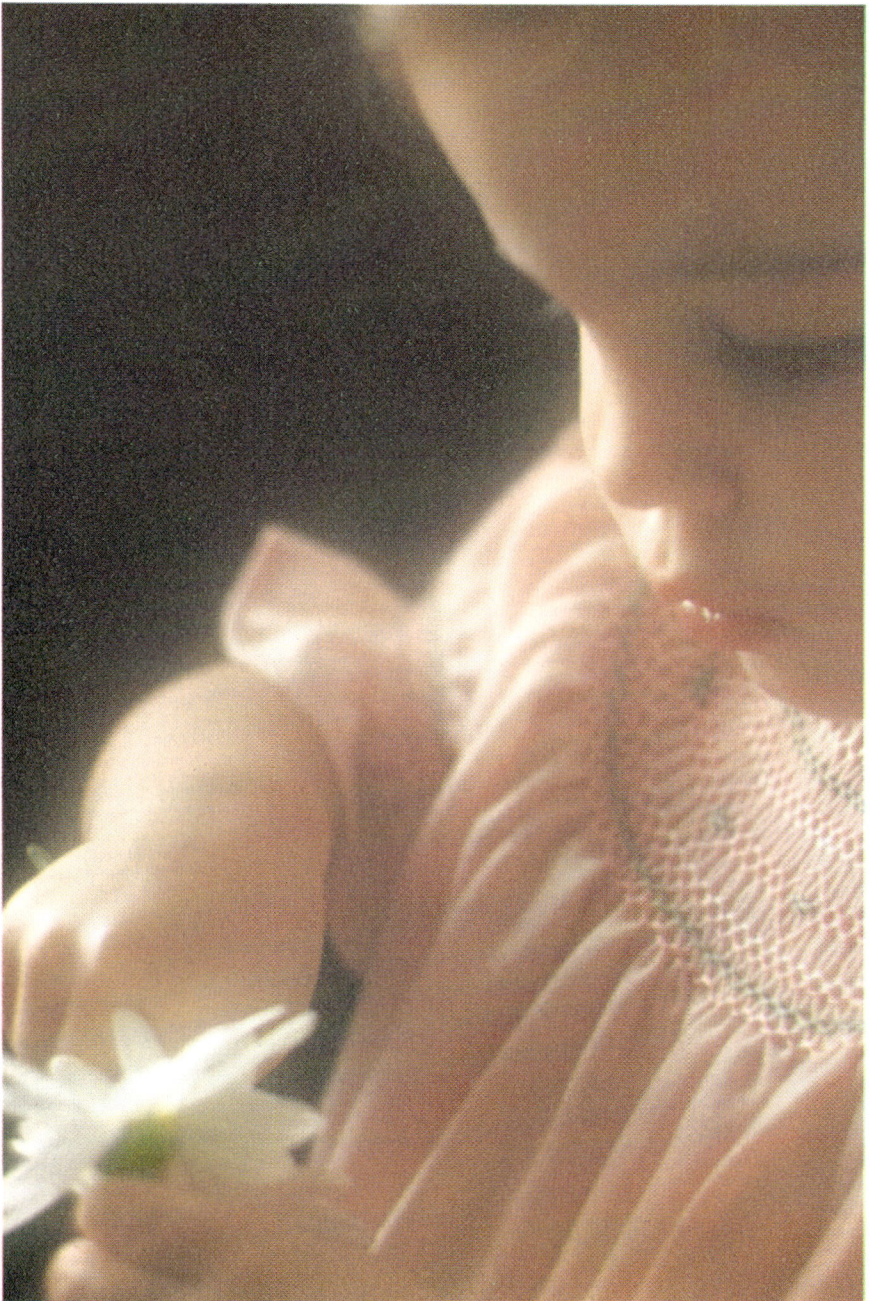

Acknowledgments

The editor and the publisher have made every effort to trace the ownership of all copyrighted material and to secure permission from copyright holders of such material. In the event of any question arising as to the use of any material the publisher and editor, while expressing regret for inadvertent error, will be pleased to make the necessary corrections in future printings. Thanks are due to the following authors, publishers, publications and agents for permission to use the material indicated.

GEORGES BORCHARDT, INC., for an excerpt from "Letter to My Grandmother" by Susan Jacoby. Originally published in the October 1977 issue of *McCall's*. Copyright © 1977 by Susan Jacoby.

THE CHRISTIAN SCIENCE MONITOR, for "The Fortune" by Norma Farber reprinted from the January 18, 1978 issue of *The Christian Science Monitor*. Copyright © 1978 by The Christian Science Publishing Society. All rights reserved. For an excerpt from "Any Age We Please" by Lee Neville reprinted from the February 7, 1978 issue. Copyright © 1978 by The Christian Science Publishing Society. All rights reserved.

THE CURTIS PUBLISHING COMPANY, for "From Grandmother" by LoVerne Brown. Reprinted from *The Saturday Evening Post*. Copyright © 1961 The Curtis Publishing Company.

DELACORTE PRESS, for an excerpt from "this early afternoon..." reprinted from *Make A Circle, Keep Us In* by Arnold Adoff. Copyright © 1975 by Arnold Adoff.

DOUBLEDAY & COMPANY, INC., for an excerpt from *At Wit's End* by Erma Bombeck. Copyright © 1965, 1966, 1967 by Newsday, Inc.

DOWNE PUBLISHING, INC., for "But Oh! With Love" by Gladys McKee Iker reprinted from the August 1974 issue of the *Ladies' Home Journal*. Copyright © 1974 by Gladys McKee Iker.

M. EVANS & COMPANY, INC., for an excerpt from *In Search of Myself and Other Children* by Eda LeShan. Copyright © 1976 by Eda J. LeShan.

FARRAR, STRAUS & GIROUX, INC., for an excerpt from *The Summer of the Great-Grandmother* by Madeleine L'Engle. Copyright © 1974 by Crosswicks, Ltd.

GARRARD PUBLISHING CO., for "What Grandma Says" by B. J. Lee from *Hello People* by Leland B. Jacobs. Copyright © 1972 by Leland B. Jacobs.

GROSSET & DUNLAP, INC., for "The House Plants" and "When Grandmama Was Young" from *The Sparrow Bush* by Elizabeth Coatsworth. Copyright © 1966 by Grosset & Dunlap, Inc. British Commonwealth rights granted by the author.

HARPER & ROW, PUBLISHERS, INC., for an excerpt from *A Joyful Noise* by Janet Gillespie. Copyright © 1971 by Janet Gillespie.

HOUGHTON MIFFLIN COMPANY, for an excerpt from *Smashed Potatoes: A Kid's Eye View of the Kitchen* edited by Jane G. Martel. Copyright © 1974 by Jane G. Martel.

ALFRED A. KNOPF, INC., for "Velvet Shoes" from *Collected Poems of Elinor Wylie* by Elinor Wylie. Copyright © 1921 by Alfred A. Knopf, Inc. and renewed 1949 by William Rose Benet.

ROBERT LESCHER LITERARY AGENCY, for an excerpt from "What Grandparents Can Give" by Dr. Benjamin Spock. Copyright © 1971. John D. Houston II, Trustee.

J. B. LIPPINCOTT COMPANY, for an excerpt from *The Stillmeadow Road* by Gladys Taber. Copyright © 1962 by Gladys Taber.

MARY MUNGER LUKE, for an excerpt from "G Is For Grandmother" reprinted from the January 1978 issue of the *Berkshire Sampler*.

MACMILLAN PUBLISHING CO., INC., for three excerpts from *A Book For Grandmothers* by Ruth Goode. Copyright © 1976 by Ruth Goode. British Commonwealth rights granted by Curtis Brown, Ltd. (New York); for excerpts from *Sixpence In Her Shoe* by Phyllis McGinley. Copyright © 1960, 1962, 1963, 1964 by Phyllis McGinley. British Commonwealth rights granted by Curtis Brown, Ltd. (London).

WILLIAM MORRIS AGENCY, INC., for an excerpt from "Meditations for the Suburban Woman" by Gwen Davis. Copyright © 1976 by Gwen Davis.

THE NEW YORK TIMES COMPANY, for excerpts from "Hugs, Kisses & Chicken Soup" by Florence D. Shelley reprinted from an early May 1978 issue of *The New York Times*. Copyright © 1978 by The New York Times Company.

READER'S DIGEST, for excerpts from "The Lady Who Lived Through Winter" by Joan Mills reprinted from the April 1974 issue.

CHARLES SCRIBNER'S SONS, for "Children and Other Creatures" by Felice Holman. Copyright © 1970 by Felice Holman.

SIMON & SCHUSTER, for an excerpt from "What Is A Grandmother" by Lee Parr McGrath and Joan Scobey. Copyright © 1970 by Lee Parr McGrath and Joan Scobey.

BETTIE PAYNE WELLES, for "Love" from *Nantucket House* by Bettie Payne Welles. Reprinted from the February 1978 issue of *The Pen Woman*.

Photo Credits:

Gary Carpenter—cover; Steven Mack—cover; Elizabeth Welsh—p. 2; Jeffrey Munk—p. 6; James Patrick—pp. 10, 23, 42; Three Lions, Inc.—p. 15; Jane Novak—p. 19; Peter Clemens—pp. 30, 51; Four by Five, Inc.—pp. 27, 38, 55; Pat Powers—p. 35; John Taylor— p. 47.

Selected by Barbara Shook Hazen
Designed by Thomas James Aaron
Set in Palatino